American Boy

by Dean Smith

Washington Writers' Publishing House
Washington, D.C.

ACKNOWLEDGMENTS

Poems appearing in *American Boy* have been published in *Poetry East, Open City, Gulf Coast, Charlotte Review, The Pearl, Cultural Studies Times,* and *Big Wednesday Review*. Additional work has been anthologized in *Beyond Lament: An Anthology of Holocaust Poetry* and is forthcoming in *Fresh Water*.

For Brendan Macauley Smith

Photo courtesy of Kerry Dean Touchette

Publication of this book is possible thanks to donations from the many Friends of Washington Writers' Publishing House.

Copyright © 2000 Dean Smith
All rights reserved.
Printed in the United States of America.

Library of Congress Cataloging-in-Publication Data

Washington Writers' Publishing House
P.O. Box 15271   Washington, D.C. 20003

Contents

I. Home Movies

Last Day of Kindergarten 3
Lucky Ones 4
Druid Hill, 1969 5
Head Fake 6
Loch Raven Reservoir 7
Wedding Photograph, 1963 8
Home Movies 9
Chow Mein 11
Red Crayon 12
Wrecked 13
Quisp vs. Quake 16
Greeting Sister Liam, 1971 18
Hollywood Kiss 19
Waiting for You 20
Roller Coaster 21
Sailing to St. Michaels 22
Black Pond 23
Four Italian Uncles 24
Mary Loretta Swift Remembered 25
Kite 27
Black Winter 29

II. Tectonics

Quarrier 33
Eleanora 34
Listen to the Bird 37
Zona Blues 38
Remember 39
Pea Soup 42
Chesapeake Blue 43
Remains 46

III. SKIN DIVER

After Two Years *51*
Obsession *52*
Skin Diver *53*
No Escaping *54*
The Wound *55*
Postcards *56*
Old Timer *57*
Still Life with Paper *58*
Anastasia *59*
Epilogue *62*
Sea Rocks, Monterosso *64*
Thin Ledge, Nearing Vernazza *65*
Vertigo, Approaching Corniglia *66*
Sauce from Scratch, Manarola *67*
Last Words, Riomaggiore *68*

I. Home Movies

"I look about wildly."
—James Wright

Last Day of Kindergarten

The janitor locks the schoolhouse door.
Rusted swings creak in the breeze,
I keep watch for a maroon Corvair.

Dusk unrolls across the playground
like a cigarette-burned rug.
A wooden train roars
into the shadows.

I twist a Nehi can in half,
stack my finger painting in the sandbox:
spitfires and destroyers war
against a blue-green sky.

In the classrooms, switches flick off.
My glow-in-the-dark watch
reads almost time for *Mod Squad*.
Maybe she doesn't want me anymore.

At last, mom pulls up to the gate.
I run to show her the red stars on my papers
but she's still in her nightgown.

She's sorry she forgot to pick me up,
watching television all day
because Bobby Kennedy was shot.
Tears on her cheek taste like the ocean.

Lucky Ones

B-52 strikes and Oriole scores
riddle the morning paper.
All day in the woods pinned
with medals from an ex-marine
who kept a rattlesnake head on his dresser,
we aim our plastic M-16s.

GI Joe returned three inches tall
scrapped like the Mustangs
Chevys and Buicks
he worked on in the driveway
under a bedroom decorated
with trophies and pennants
from outcomes more safely decided.

On a slanted granite slab
off Lincoln's left foot
sixty thousand soldiers etched
in gray along a narrow walk
rest silently in formation.

War-torn stares reach
beyond the parallel
into spaces reserved for MIAs,
persistent and indelible,
and others still to come
streaked in residues
of napalm, Agent Orange.

Snapshots, altars of dog tags,
fallen dominoes bring back memories
for lucky ones who laughed, played dead.

Druid Hill, 1969

Our last family trip to the zoo was on a Sunday in knee-highs and saddle shoes on swings under the big oaks of late summer in eight millimeter we all looked swell together among ostriches and orangutans and at the art exhibit zeroing in on a woman with every inch of her skin spinning her web of indifference to cameras catching tree priests and beatniks circling the amazing Technicolor Volkswagen beetle parked at the House of Reptiles where *savoir faire* was everywhere amongst the peddlers flush with matted monarch wings and love beads blowing glass and selling peace in my parents last year together before the nation did a cannonball off the high dive and great notions like families went out of fashion with the wicker furniture Dad packed into the U-Haul leaving us scratched versions of "Are You Experienced?" and "Beggar's Banquet."

Mom dressed us like Kennedy children keeping her framed collages of Dr. King, Kahlil Gibran, and Rod McKuen working two jobs against the silent majority in the blue collar bouffant & buzz cut Baltimore army scene a stronghold since Francis Scott Key scribbled his anthem for shift workers hammering iron to build the heartland at Sparrows Point feeding a war machine economy at Aberdeen with bombers, tanks, and napalm impervious to the violence at Altamont or a far away jungle where children ran from villages sacrificed in defoliant showers and my parents on their last night together strafed the walls with intermittent fire until the clicking strand of film snapped on that old projector Dad won in an Esso sales contest.

Head Fake

On a back door give-and-go,
he left our house to coach
in Wheeling, West Virginia.

No harm. No foul,
I learned to shoot on the perimeter
against Bazooka Joe, an invisible defender
at the end of an alley, where the fundamentals
of separation became the head fake,
the spin-move, the jab step,
aggressive, tenacious
when I found the range
to play for him
and hit the open jumper
somewhere off the turnpike
in a frigid January gym.

After twelve years of chasing
a basketball dream,
he traded his whistle for real estate.
I rode the bench at St. Ignatius Loyola,
hung the high tops
on a nail outside Chicago,
more a man for others
than a serious hoop threat
when I discovered
basketball is love,
requires a soft touch
from long range.

Loch Raven Reservoir

Pierced by a hook a worm is a lure
under a bridge humming with cars. We cast

off on a lark to scare up the blennies.
Nothing all morning save lump fish and trash

on that mud-veined bank. Maryland waters
might redeem us with striped bass, sunfish, or carp.

Sprung from months at Pleasant Plains Elementary,
we dared each other to jump.

My rod curled against the pull of the waterfall.
Sneakers leaden with muck, I yanked it back

and forth along the edge, fell in the water.
Skilled in the ways of untangling, a fisherman

clucked, "Rip the string, surrender bobber and hook."
My last. Determined to gut it out, I never gave up.

Then the snag rose extended from the shell
of a giant snapper, jaws clamped on the bait,

beak coming out of the water toward me.

Wedding Photograph, 1963

Outside St. Ursula's
a worried nun clamps
you both together
in the trap of her habit,
prays the marriage will stick
on short notice.
An extra veil and dress
hang suspended
above your head,
reserved for a virgin
in the double exposure
keeping another engagement.
A morning suit hovers over him
stolen from his best friend,
now an ex-fiance
out of the picture
serving his country.
The groom looks confident
like Johnny Unitas,
among the masses
gathered quickly to witness
another miraculous comeback.
Your smile exposes
the wonders of Tuscany,
but this is East Baltimore, and underneath
the roses in your gloved hands
my unexpected feet kick.

Home Movies

*"The radio played dirges, requiems, hymns of sadness.
a feeling of emptiness spread."*
　　　　　—*Baltimore Sun,* November 23, 1963

Abraham the dressmaker started shooting
through the telephoto lens
of his Bell & Howell Zoomatic camera
when the motorcade turned the corner.

I was taken to see "Alice in Wonderland"
in swaddling clothes at Mercy High School,
to witness my aunt's first big theatrical role.

Abraham wasn't going to bring it
but his secretary convinced him
to capture twenty-six seconds of history.

My mother didn't want a baby in '63,
my father on his knees begged her to leave
the abortion clinic on Greenmount Avenue.

He captured signs, trees, and Governor Connolly,
the last of the filler takes before the procession,
tracking lead cycles out of the frame.

Mom believed in John-John, Jacqueline,
and the New Frontier enough
to love him for the time being, give birth to me.

Abraham heard the crack, thought the Chief
was playing a game as he leaned
over to tell Jacqueline: "Oh, they got me."

Outside the delivery room, my father found her bleeding
through the lens of his brand new eight millimeter.
JFK spoke of world peace that day in September.

Another bullet whizzed over the camera
into the frame and he started crying,
"They killed him, They killed him."

An usher found us good seats close to the stage,
the house lights went down, and the curtain opened.
A breathless voice crackled over the loudspeaker.

Abraham thought police were coming for his film
when they ran past him toward the fence line,
thought someone ganged up on the President.

"President Kennedy has been shot in Dallas."
Lockers slammed everywhere outside the auditorium,
footsteps stampeding through corridors.

JFK waved from the underpass in Ray-Bans,
his initials to be used for highways, stadiums, hotels.
Reels of film strewn all over Dallas like brains.

I was sixty days old when a nun snatched me away,
cradled me past uniformed girls slumped against lockers,
ripped from umbilical cords, screaming for pacifiers.

Chow Mein

Covered in crunchy thorns
it languished on the plate
awaiting my father.

We devoured ravioli from cans,
Swanson TV dinners
in our footed pajamas
watching *The Guns of Will Sonnet*.

She blew nervous smoke
out the French doors
until the phone rang
from the Old Trail Saloon.
She whispered,
"When are you coming home?"

It stayed until morning
with the good silver
under a chandelier.

Before work, she flushed it
down the disposal,
threw away our fortunes.

The uneaten dinner
led to divorce, space at the table.
Each time I see chow mein
my stomach turns.
Chinese food has never
agreed with me.

Red Crayon

She sweeps glass into a dust pan,
rips pictures of her wedding,

cries the same way she does
when we take my brother for needles.

I listen with a red crayon
and a coloring book.

They whisper now, no screaming.
Dishes smash against the wall.

Drawers open, suitcases zip.
I'm coloring in walls, floors, windows, doors,

my brother wheezes next to me.
I pretend to be sleeping

when she comes to tell me
my father is leaving.

I walk to the window, break
the red stick between my fingers.

The sound of his engine
hums in the distance.

Pages fall to the grass,
reach the street by dawn.

Wrecked

1.

It was always more than just going away,
the night I waited on my pillow in the basement
packed up and ready for my parents
to take me down the ocean, watching a movie.

Indians attacked a hovel in the darkness
flaming arrows through the cabin window,
cries of massacre.

They were talking in the bedroom.
The movie ended and my mother
didn't want to go.

2.

In the Stardust Motel,
Ocean City, Maryland
he came with us, a regular fixture
still in love with her,

more for appearances on the roller coaster ride
at Jolly Roger, to flip the pancakes
and cram in the stall of the snapshot booth,
on the beach disgruntled, a good father, roasting.

Under the blue lights of a diner on the boardwalk
we ate apple pie and ice cream in the rain
while they slugged it out upstairs in the hotel room.
The Tilt-o-Whirl all closed up, we drove back home.

3.

"The worst one in seven years at least," she said.
A veteran of inclement weather, as if it were a hurricane
or snowstorm with everyone running for cover
when the door slammed and locked by accident
young wood ripped too soon from the hinge,
an angry man here to beat the shit out of her again.

He fought hard to save it this time,
in his underwear with the child asleep
because he loved her, I'm sure
but she never gave him the chance
swearing he tried to strangle her,
neck veins bulging as she screamed.

On the steps in the morning she cried
and we carried out the belongings:
all the new Swedish furniture,
after only two weeks in the seaside abode.
She hadn't even walked on the beach.

On the verge of extinction with the osprey,
her third husband pondered his next decision.

4.

After all the crabs were eaten or thrown out,
the red wine and deck chairs tossed into the fray,
I asked him, "Dad, can you take me to play Skee-ball?"

Wooden balls leapt furiously into hoops
and matters were steady again.
Together we walked into the arcade,
the outcome of his final toss
still in the balance, hours away.

A life preserver of diversion
his only survival today,
they walk along the ocean:
giver of driftwood to the shore,
sting of the jellyfish, horseshoe crab,
monk seal and humpback whale,
spreading out across the sand.

She changed her mind and it all flowed back inside:
broken toys, chandelier, rocking chair,
the plankton of our lives sent back
into the feeding chain,
ocean.

Quisp vs. Quake

Rival boxes faced off on the table.
A cross-eyed Martian,
propeller on head,
a burly miner in hardhat and spikes,
introduced as war escalated
were more than just
breakfast cereal
eaten with my father.

Quisp stood for the Lunar mission
oat-flavored flying saucers
carrying Armstrong & Aldrin
looked like contact lenses,
tasted of space exploration.

Quisp piloted balloons we sent
from second grade,
that ended up in Ohio
tagged for the moon.
Sugar-coated toys
flew from our balcony
made for a nice surprise.

An Anglo-Norman invader
in need of make-over,
Quake posed a serious threat
in his earth-digger car,
launched bits of cereal
from a back seat catapult,
the transition from hard hat
to Australian cowboy not enough
to dispel his war-like nature.

Given the billing of Ali vs. Frazier
the brute aggressor that tasted better
was no match for a techno-wizard.

I ripped up his undershirts before work.
Quisp won the popularity contest.
Quake went MIA like my father.
I missed them both in the morning.

Greeting Sister Liam, 1971

You came to our house for dinner
after a ten-year stint under the habit.
At the door, I showed no mercy:
"Green isn't your color."

I didn't know you planned
to defect from the convent,
purchase lace boots, mini-skirts,
marry my father.

Crushed in the hall,
your favorite dress
permanently stained
by a six-year old kid.

In truth, the verdant hue
is the perfect compliment
to your classic Kelly beauty.

But not on that afternoon,
your freckles another story.

Hollywood Kiss

Hanging on the edge of the hospital bed,
she watches the odd sleep of a man with one arm.

He told her an elephant bit it off.
Now, he can't open his eyes.

In a cold vinyl hospital chair
she remembers being thirteen,

led to his room to watch Johnny Carson.
She pushed him off in the blue glow of a Zenith

but one strong arm held a secret she could not understand.
Her grandmother always slept downstairs,

a rosary coiled on her bedside table.
She went to him in a trance,

part of a routine, as easy as their afternoon walk
into town for cherry snow balls.

The grandchild whose dreams they made fun of
became an actress on television.

How strange it felt when she first made love,
dabbing her blood on a page of Edna St. Vincent Millay.

She waits for him to die in this sterile room
adorned with her roses, clutching a lifeless hand.

Each labored breath approaches forgiveness.

Waiting for You

Gritty red brick row home,
outskirts of Baltimore
circa the second coming,
I'll look through the stained glass between us
while my victrola scratches "Exile on Main Street."

Saturday morning around my way
children tear down the alley,
a lewd cacophony smeared
with a mix of dirt, ice cream.
Mamas spend the day in curlers
watching *Bowling for Dollars*.

Obsolete papas scrape mustard
from their backfins, over cases
of National Bohemian.

Working the night shift on a loading dock
with a forklift full of broken hearts,
space on my arm for a flamingo tattoo,
I'll wait until you grace these marble steps.

Roller Coaster

I loved all of them: Hershey Park, Steel Pier
and the Maryland State Fair.

I couldn't wait to get my ticket,
strap in, scream like a wild man.

It's taken seven years to get to the top of this incline
the rickety wood cringes, paint chips off the beams.

A swirl of air at the top of the plunge
screams of gears and grease. I hold on

with both hands, afraid to look.

Sailing to St. Michaels

Loosed from cleats off Crockett's boatyard,
Victoria drags a slade across deserted shallows

in the drizzle of early November. Shotgun shells bob
from the marshes in a scatter of feathers.

Our engine stills for a great blue heron.
Skipjacks and oysterboats rock to the side.

Camouflage voices waft from the blind,
Victoria slows on a drab linen of water and sky.

Hail pelts the Choptank River,
Cormorants scour the fringes.

Mergansers woggle to St. Michaels.
Orange bills strut down cobblestone lanes.

Swans and buffleheads make up our landing party.
Hunters flock in the rain outside Perry Cabin.

The lobby throngs with pheasants, gulls, and peacocks
coiffed in flight across a paneled sky.

The russet beards of watermen brood
On seasons of illegal dumping.

Their ice chests are stuffed with Canada geese.
Cannons of thunder boom over the marshes.

Black Pond

Swing out across the water on sweaty August afternoons
twisting on the rope swing until the last possible second:

catapulted into the center of the lake, the cold bottom water
draws your feet closer to whatever's buried underneath.

Sink into blackness, past quarry dead floating
with their quartz teeth: accidentally drowned at picnics,

the stockings and brassieres of burlesque queens,
shattered husks clinging to their garments,

snuffed-out bookies and flimflam artists, bodies
the divers never found, all down in a potter's field of county bones,

drifters from other towns, nickel-plated pistols used in murders,
those liar-cheater-stealer secrets like anchors that sink

us to the floor of the kettle-hole, broken, flat on our backs,
staring up from the mire at the swans moving silently across

bellies of catfish, swimmers who thrash until dark,
the lithe dance of a copperhead, fragile perch of an egret,

the prehistoric span of a heron's flight caressing the world.
See yourself on the bottom from the Great Blue's eye,

thrusting upward like a rocket into sunlit milk and rise
into woodrot and buttonbush, dripping like a newborn

over moss-covered rungs, jumping off again.

Four Italian Uncles

Mario recovered from a stroke:
booze, pills, and nicotine.
He broke out of Miami General
for Lucky Strikes and a Scotch.

The nurse strapped him down again.
He lapsed into a coma.

Floozies and ex's slugged
it out at the funeral home.
He slept through it all.

Renato died a war hero years ago.
Sergio went to the dog track.
Dino stayed home.

Mary Loretta Swift Remembered

Nana bought me my first baseball glove,
a Mickey Lolich autographed Spalding,
from Pop's Toy Shop
next to Hoschild Kohn
after her hair was done.

On weekends, we stayed up late
watching *Creature Feature* and *Mannix*.
On the phone with Pop-pop
the night I vanished behind the pull-out,
she thought she lost me.

I slept in the curl of her legs,
her golden hair on a satin pillow.
On Sunday mornings, up early,
in her chair watching me sleep,
whispering, "Good morning, hon."

He appeared toothless at noon
crotch undone in his pajamas,
the legs of a sprinter shocking white.
He wanted pancakes.

"God Save Us and Love Us,
this knife can't cut hot butter."

I slammed tennis balls
against her walls, pretended
Orioles were involved.
She let me do what I wanted,
collect pen-knives and switchblades,
pursue vermin with homemade traps
of American cheese, wood glue.

We went out for snowballs,
spent weekends talking religion,
how God didn't mean for children
to have more than one mother
after my parents were finished.

Pop-pop once left her in a ditch
wearing Final Net and Jean Nate
on the way to a party.
He was already out dating
after she was told
terminal cancer.

Kite

The roll flew out of my hand.
Brendan dove head first, caught the twine
before it tumbled into the ocean.
A routine rescue mission.

The time he pushed a stalled car
across the train tracks, the driver accidentally wounded,
a locomotive barreling into the station.

Brendan fashioned a tourniquet
from a sweat sock, made the front page
of the *Glencoe News*.

When the seizures came,
I could never touch him
as he writhed on the floor, turning blue.

The voice of the operator
dangled in the air next to me.
I snapped like kite string.

We buried our grandmother
three days ago.

The speck rose out over the ocean
with the soul of Mary Swift
on her way back to Shannon.

At dusk, I flew the bird, lost it again.
Brendan gone for Chicago.

I trudged back through the prickers,
wound string around my fist,

already missing my brother.
I could never tell him what happened:

how I stood motionless,
when the bird broke free again.

I made no attempt to save them:
my brother, a kite, a marriage.

I found the kite
in the driveway
of our summer home.

Black Winter

Learn the way of a Blackhawk warrior.
His first few months in an oxygen tent,
the doctors spiked his arms with penicillin.
He walked forty perches on the sheets of Lake Michigan.

Ice rafts steam into the tundra's sky,
winter drives its tarpaulins over a hero in WWI.
The brother of Archibald MacLeish is buried
a furlong from my window.

The Winnetka police brought him home again.
He slept through another convulsion.
I saw the gods strangle him, then disappear.
My mother called a reputable brain surgeon.

Blackhawks burrow into bearskin and fire.
He wants to play football on the medication.
Wind throws ice against the glass around him.
He dreams of open field tackles, panes wincing.

II. TECTONICS

Quarrier

The cavern widens
and pressures rise into granite schist.

Pressed against a solid face,
I chisel walls for stones, finger knots

of secret histories suspended alone
above the quarry at nightfall.

Plates move inside me like ice
across a freezing pond,

pent-up gasses release.
The slightest shift will drop me back

through the lines, across a generation
of digging men, into the center of things.

Snowball garnets echo the language
of lava cooling down newly formed ranges,

cataclysmic pain. Magma surges
into my fault zones, darkness sweeps

across the hardening mausoleums of canyon.
Granite serves the dead, its interlocking

mesh details a journey back to the rind.
Our pickaxe voices in the ash

swirl up from the bottom, scrape
down the rock into a groove.

Eleanora

1.
Like a blue-tailed fly,
stripped down, humming through air,
she left me years ago

in the falling water of sheets
where we didn't move for days

making love in a cathode pool
of television, Jell-O molds, innocence

stoned on horseback, missing gigs,
our spiked neon veins entwined

in a locket of cheap hotels.
She was my lady then,

half Cherokee, half Irish,
high cheekbones, warrior priestess.

What's thrown away will come back
to haunt you like a stiff joint

in the low palm flicked
between the jetties.

I hated to leave her place:
the brightness of sun on palm trees,

sea birds' screech and crotchety wail,
slim trail of a salamander

across a parched sidewalk.
It could be anywhere:

Winnemucca, Rock Springs,
Lovelock.

2.

Eleanora's time under house arrest,
freshly poured suburbia lobotomizing slowly.

Her last public performance: Phoenix Theatre, 1959.
She vanished into the dust of Nevada

into the fumes of night,
into high beams like tumbleweed

into the languid steam of a radiator.
Shredded souls at dusk float

above the cathedral still hanging on,
a voice like slow love grinding

into many orgasms. Starving in Harlem,
she hustled for chump change.

Don't let a voice like that
go somewhere in the rain.

Her riffs cracked skulls
past corroded hotels, deserted gas stations.

Fellow musicians left in tears like dead goats
splayed on an asphalt shoulder.

Laramie sky, red rocks, thunderhead.
Absence is what drives us across the high plains.

3.
I search for her everywhere
in the lonely freight of the Union Pacific,

across a desert track where I can taste the salt air
for fifty miles on the sodium drag strip of Utah.

There's still something obscene
about making love in a Motel Six.

During a push start in Lovelock,
the sky fills with coyote teeth.

Nothing survives for long here:
high beam, low beam, dust balls leaping.

The guards stayed in her room for hours
to make sure she was dead.

A robin's egg blue Cadillac
in the tall grass, spectacular fins alive,

let me take you somewhere
stripped down, humming through air.

I can see the house from here.
A woman unfurls into the breeze,

ripples of flag cupping her buttocks
at the sides, bronze hips spin

from a dangling cloth: mountains rise
across her beams, flushed in a throttle of gasoline,

flags, women, dreams.
What's lost makes you burn more evenly.

Listen to the Bird

and to Dizzy at Rick's Café American
ballooning his cheeks for "A Night in Tunisia"
in the city of the big shoulders.

To the muted pet of Marsalis
lifting a world unto his lips
an uptown ruler introduced with,
"You can call me anything but fabulous,"
spouting the discourse of human intercourse,
all the way up the lamp post in mid-winter.

You hear birds in the afternoon
on 23rd and Broadway, the zweet, zweet,
abduction of time by traffic horns.
Shorter plays some kind of *Yankee Doodle Meets Godzilla*
the night we bombed Libya, and Chet couldn't read the music
but made love to it, a different genus, species specific.
Thrumming on the corner in the lush life mainline
of Charlie Parker, that shit was *badderthanamotherfucker*
and Miles to go into the veins of the sky.

Space fills with slick saxophone religion.
Soul as organ grinder *thickerthangumbo*
sucks blood from a pump
nightcrawling out of its moonlit skin,
the power of birds, hoodoo snake charmers,
scrub it clean and sharp from the bone.

Everybody knows trombone players never get laid,
sliding it home and back again,
listen to the birds, to the heavy weather.

Charlie blows his flugel horn and it's nice
brings him back from the dead.

Zona Blues

Rising out of the ash pits,
out of the mudflats and reservations,
pampas, shopping malls, and driving ranges,
resurrected fast food chains,
Sizzler, I-hop, and the deadly Jack-in-the-Box,
out of the missing teeth of high-rises erected on quicksand
across a lavender sky drift Navaho, Pima, Apache
carved into red rocks, souls and the charred bits of their bones
scattered in the exhaust fumes, clogged
in snarling engines at sundown,
their descendants penned in and given tools
to immolate themselves with firewater,
casinos, and revolvers, as in *Juego de las Pelotas*
when the losers are sacrificed to *El Serpiente Emplumada*,
inhaling cremation fumes like burnt steak of geriatrics
from the Midwest laid to rest with their fortunes flushed
in the slot machine toilets of Las Vegas and nothing
better to do than settle down on the listless grunge
of the southwest, where two-bit lizard kings wallow
in witness protection programs and this episode of *COPS*
is live from the prefab adobe huts of Phoenix.

The smell of mesquite settles on the Gila Mountains
where armaments crouch behind the middle fingers of cacti
pointed at the muse in the sky, a bleach blond baby
sucking in the gold water lust that devoured the Indians
on the burnt trail, an oasis of blood as the eagle
takes its prey crushed in the grill of an Eldorado,
ready to feed on itself and not a body to be found
in this outpost of the dead on the underbelly
of the nation where sandstone cliff dwellings
glow with televisions in a beautiful abyss at sunset.

Remember
for C. McGrath

Santa Ana crossed the Rio Grande
toward a stone pinata stuffed
with Jim Bowie and Davy Crockett.
His iguanas gleamed in rows
over an anonymous earth
thirsting for sacrificial blood.

From a crumbling adobe mission,
snipers picked off the soldiers at will
in their little boy blue uniforms,
a threatening affliction on the horizon,
growing stronger by the thousands,
the fort rationing its ammunition.

Santa Ana's call for surrender
answered by a cannonball:
no casualties sustained
in the first three days
by the Texans of San Antonio de Padua,
a hotbox of admirals, renegades, mountain men,
killers from all over the country.

Frontiersman in a murderous whorl
of single shot rifle and tomahawk;
ripped, hacked, and bashed through the ranks
schooled in the American wilderness
bear killers, coon hunters, Indian slayers
wiping out entire divisions.

Dying of fever, Bowie on his deathbed
a revolver in one hand
underneath the bed sheet,
the knife that made him famous
in the other, tossed on bayonets
around the courtyard.

Crockett backed into a corner,
found in a pile of seventeen dead Mexicans, killers
larger than life itself, old friend
Sam Houston unavailable for comment,
on a political mission.

John Wayne directed an epic retelling,
pure history in the making,
Widmark's Bowie hungover and pissed off,
a midnight raid to steal a cannon,
yucking it up at the cantina.

Frankie Avalon went to get help,
the events inside the mission
enough to make you cry
when Bowie and Crockett die,
the Mexican army collapsing
into the dust of the camera
by the battalions.

The Duke rose from the carnage
in a chartered jet, king of the rhubarb
with a heart bigger than America itself,
ruler of the charnel house.
A buckskin deity capable
of righting all wrongs
in Cuba, Indochina,
and Red Square.

Sunset on the garrison along the back wall
sharp light against sandstone
a slight wind that never gives in
to the artifacts of bombardment:
combs, razors, Colt .45s.

It was a rare breed that shared
the motto, down one hundred to one:
"Give me victory, or give me death,"
without a prayer in the violent birth of Texas.

Pea Soup

The connoisseurs of pea soup pay homage
to the famous chef of the green larvae exhibition.
In his honor, all the diners serve pea soup.

Followers of sacred gruel wearing bibs
bring their customized ladles
to the all-you-can-eat cauldron.
It has been known to stain.

They huddle around heaping bowls of slime,
slurp like there's no tomorrow.
It gathers in green law-abiding lumps.

In Japan it's a delicacy.
I like minestrone, chowder, cream of mushroom.
They will never stop eating.

I peer through the window,
see bowls of radioactive fluid
for breakfast, lunch, and dinner.

Chesapeake Blue

I swim sideways to claw a chicken neck,
beady eyes lodged in the netting,
trapped for centuries and dumped
into a cast iron pot.

I scrap until my pincers slow,
tight-roping over backfins
stacked in a cauldron. Raised flamenco
fisticuffs relax under an avalanche
of National Bohemian,
rocksalt, Old Bay seasoning.

Steam cooks my meat into delicacy
of Patapsco or "backwater,"
my black eyes roll forward and back,
devour glittering plankton of history.

I burrow into a land mass granted
by King Charles to Lord Baltimore,
my empty husks traded by Nanticoke
to the British with tobacco.

I cling to the bottom of clipper ships
supplied for revolution: fifteen-hundred bombs
in twenty-four hours exploding.

A brittle, crab-like tenacity dips
cannon balls in hot grease,
gives birth to a nation in the Battle of 1814.

Plug-uglies quaff ales, pelt the Union regiment
with rocks at Camden Station,
massacred in flintlock fire.

At Sharpsburg and Antietam,
we claw on both sides,
families divided by regional tides.

Influx of German, Irish, and Italian
their blue-collar faith buttressed
by rows of marble steps scrubbed

and shining with tank-top pride,
balancing craps and boilermakers,
gnattering about Orioles.

Miss Lily the burlesque queen performs
her routines for Baltimore gentlemen,
swigging Black Label in the Light Street Lounge.

I stab and squeeze the drowned cigars
of H.L. Mencken, flicked from harbor side,
his squat reflection in my rolling eyes.

Cab Calloway, Eubie Blake, and Billie Holiday
sizzle like crab cakes on Pennsylvania Avenue
working the Aurora and the Club Royal.

Zelda sets Shepherd Pratt on fire
while F. Scott Fitzgerald burns the midnight oil
with Gertrude Stein on Bolton Hill.

Soft shells, silver queen, and snowballs
flourish in the counties at crab feasts,
newspapers covering the table.

Mallets pound and crack to pluck
the precious meat until my carapace
is scraped for mustard and stacked.

My pronged land mass squeezes Chesapeake
between its claws, shallow heated basin
stocked with jumbo crabs rising into nets

to stab a chicken neck, the largest annual catch
from Sparrow's Point to Havre de Grace
Catoctin Mountain to Sweet Air.

I dream in winter shoals, alluvial folds
fringed with bays and estuaries
of crab mother, earth.

Remains

Implements of torture
loom above the village

on display from the time of Luther
reserved for heretics, witches,

peasant rebellion.
In the Hacker's Chair,

a throne of spikes
also known as Maiden's Womb,

wooden needles prick
a sorceress with bad impressions.

The Schadleknacker or "headcrusher"
tightens a vise on radical heads

shortens the distance from skull-top to chin.
The Sage, or saw, with two handles

on either side of the prisoner
who straddles the blade

hung upside down alive
until the teeth reach sternum.

Rack, saw, guillotine
and the residue that clings.

These crude devices
can't compare to their

counterparts at Auschwitz
Bergen-Belsen, Dachau:

an industrialization of hatred
in the nozzles of showers,

the enlarged mouths of crematoria
designed to fit more bodies in,

genius turned inward upon life.
Unable to sleep tonight with news

of a Molotov attack on a party
of immigrants in Stuttgart,

faint reminders of ovens, poisonous gas,
dreams gathered in piles

along with shoes, clothes, lives.
Indelible wounds, bandaged by time, open fresh.

III. SKIN DIVER

After Two Years

I hold you in the sizzle of the rain,
kiss the scars that lace your skin,

as ivy spreads across the leaded glass,
framing us in leafy strands.

I can't grasp what lies beyond the darkness,
or what we look like sprawled together

from the trees, when dreams creep
between our sleeping bodies,

wrap us tightly here forever.

Obsession

I think of you at night on a frozen lake
untouchable, wrapped in a bear shawl.

Your dogsled undone.
Zephyrs waltzing around you.

A face as naked as anything
on the moon-skinned ice.

One step farther and a crack
extends into the horizon.

The lake, like an old door, aches
with desperation.

We collapse in the shards of no tomorrow.
Lust of the water, press of the sky.

Skin Diver

I dive into the ruins of an underwater city
searching between rocks for a shell

that keeps a perfect hardness under wraps.
I wedge it open slowly, in case

the secret washes from the folds
into a coral village.

Today, she is an empty smile,
while my shadow ripples across

the bottom like a stingray,
and pearls of breath

flow toward the surface.

No Escaping

I wake like a fugitive,
sweating as you rest in fragile strands,

swan crushed against the side of a building.
Sharp dancer's body electric,

its searchlights and tripwires
protect my dreams from trespass.

You've choked off my garden,
tendrils at the window,

light from your reflection
saved for indoor pools.

You may never let me touch you again,
but I will remember your lithe frame at peace.

The Wound

Wrapped in seaweed,
hearts tumble into surf.

Pick them up bruised and blue,
clogged with sand.

Check for your name—no luck today.
The next shipment on the breaker line

tags glistening in the sun.
Walk this beach, I'll find it,

hole in my chest singed with air.

Postcards

Blank on the bedside table,
stamped to my lover.

After you left,
I took pictures of dogs
leaping in fountains,
interviewed the "plagiste"
about his liaisons,
wandered the old town at night
to avoid the sadness
of the empty hotel room.

I could have discussed
how we made love
for the first time in years
as mountain wind
swirled across the patio,
how the sea sucked itself from the stones,
with the shiver of your smile
when you stepped into water.

Filling in spaces: a wish
you were here, rocky beach,
weather vane.

Old Timer

I am the hardball left in the backyard
since last summer, barely visible,
waterlogged from hibernation,
ripped at the stitching. Hit hard
through dry-rotting seasons,
thousands of vulnerable rubber bands
wait for a warm hand to grip the seams again.
I'm the extra ball for batting practice
brown with grass stains,
hard enough to snap wood.

Still Life with Paper
for Ann Wilmot Gauthier

Lying in a shack on the swamp meadow
overgrown with jewelweed, curled-up
in the middle of the floor, scraped out from the inside.
This dank shed collapses on my scraps in every corner:
spittoon, Bowie knife, wood rot, rabbit trap, bent nails.

I make no indentations,
pray to the knees of a cypress
to the swamp land, help me survive,
with a little soup on the Sterno,
water, rice, crocodile eye,
Walker's ghost as my guide.

Wind rattles corrugated tin: listen for opossum,
copperhead, wild boar, the sweet trespass of storms.
I whittle down to nothing: dented mailbox, bone shack.

Anastasia

> *"Stuck around St. Petersburg,*
> *Saw it was a time for a change..."*
>   —*Sympathy for the Devil*, The Rolling Stones

Her lace fringe burns across Blue Ridge.
Purple shadows spread between columns,
tricks of perception left by Jefferson
to tease like honeysuckle on a fence.
On the Rotunda steps with two hits
of King Tut blotter, the first dogwoods
and jonquils called me from the perimeter
to explore what lingered there.
I chased a wayward raven
through Ragged Mountain,
with visions of a former life,
a defector from a rebel enterprise.
I tripped into the April moon
plunging over burrs and thorns
across the railroad tracks
through a kudzu trail of jagged rock
caught in the throat of a screaming woman.

In the front seat of a beat up Chevy wagon
half-naked and twisting in convulsion,
her mass of wrinkles and steel wool
fixed me in a quenchless gaze.
She spit and hissed like a rattler
until a screen door slammed behind a row of azaleas,
a strange man stumbled through an ivy covered arch.
"I am her husband," he said, exhuming a dusty
Coca-Cola from newspapers and rubble in the car.
Hans claimed she wanted something warm to drink.

She sucked on the rim of a dented tin cup
under a streetlight, her blue dress dipped below
the shoulder of a cool Virginia night.
She hunkered down beneath the window

as her butler shilled from the base metals
that remained to rebuild his broken queen:
"She's embarrassed to be seen like this,
the offspring of Nicholas and Alexandra,
oldest living heir to the Romanov fortune!"

Yes, and I was the Duke of Albemarle County
with an idea he might have left her dry all night
when she needed more than just the "real thing"
from this quack historian who traced genealogies
after their betrothal in Germany.

His Anastasia painted the eggs of Nikolayevna
in the garden of the Winter Palace.
Her screams ripped through soldiers
as the rest of her family was murdered,
bullets glancing off diamond-laced corsets
in a basement near Ekaterinburg.
They didn't come to take her life
but to bed her down against the knife.
A passing farmer lifted up the sash
to find her pressed against the wall,
covered in bloody plaster, the orphaned daughter
of Mother Russia left for dead.
She crawled through barbed wire spikes
under the assumed name of "Anna Anderson"
to this haven for refugees and aristocracy.

She wheezed on a torn vinyl cushion,
springs creaked lightly, churned the blood of a dynasty.
Hans invited me inside to identify
a woman buried alive amidst wheelchairs,
kitty litter strewn across the lawn of a shack
condemned by the sanitation department.
I never saw the golden shells before she returned

to Nicholas and Alexandra, made sure she
made it through the night in the station wagon.

After years of living in squalor with packs
of stray animals, sleeping in the car
before trips to visit relatives in Lynchburg,
she died three months later in a nursing home.
Hans sprinkled her ashes on Hapsburg grounds.
The investigation of a shallow pit near St. Petersburg
revealed nothing of her bones, the subject
of television specials, childrens' cartoons,
until strands of DNA from a mass grave ended her claim.
Their shack was looted of genealogies, jewels, Kandinskys.
She left me a set of eyes from the night she screamed,
lit with terror, burning through me.

Epilogue

There's a flower sticking out of the knocker,
a small daisy of hope.

I sneak in from the rain,
grab some belongings, change of clothes,

leftovers, just like it always was,
the refrigerator stacked with uneaten dinners.

A small black dog nips at my heels.
I eat forkfuls of cold pasta,

take a swig of seltzer,
like an escaped convict,

the body tired from running,
a Murphy bed on wheels across the city.

On the couch, the dog jumps in my lap,
a small wolf-like thing I love so completely.

You're caught in the storm, somewhere
in midtown, and I must move fast.

The pain in my stomach like two knives touching,
one through the lower spine, the other, into the abdomen.

I think of amaryllis in the bedroom last winter,
how it reminded me of you, broken down in the end,

wilting like a dancer past her prime.
A small bundle of your clothes on the floor

next to the bed. The dog clutches my legs
with his paws, like "Ray-Ray" the elevator man,

asking if I'm back to stay. He talks about us on breaks,
about what a sad thing it is, what a tragedy.

I hug the dog, tell him I'll always love him.
The photos switched, my toothbrush gone,

wedding rings in a dish.
I'm out for good this time,

massive rain unrelenting.
Your sadness like a death in the family.

Sea Rocks, Monterosso

"...Mention sunsets, be not silent of her eyes..."
—John Berryman, *Dream Songs*

I look into blue-green eyes at sunset,
finger scars after years apart.

Splash of foam at the end of a wave
below your knee, sinewy fishtail

from a bar glass someone hurled
as we were breaking up.

Another gash across a thigh,
sledding in your sister's dress,

I thumb along the bone-white mark.
You never felt a cut that night.

I was coupled then, you were gone,
each of us on different sheets, a bloody mess.

We survived this slash across your heart
that stops where my marriage ends.

Night opens fresh along the water's edge,
blue-green stars, trembling hands.

Thin Ledge, Nearing Vernazza

"Rapt, buoyant I was, drenched with you, your form my hidden breathing, your face fusing into mine."
—Eugenio Montale

Hiking through vineyards endlessly into sky,
eleven years without you,

my new shoes scuffed, stumbling
over lavender, rhododora, blood red poppies.

Looking down at Monterosso,
a scrabble of dwellings, blue sea,

a room where we made love again
flooded with water, sheets twisted in sweat,

our broken torsos like neglected Venus de Milos.
I caressed your freckled body with oil,

lost territories I once explored: mountains, grasses, fiords.
We stopped for kisses, your lips fresh linguini.

A farmer called us *pomiciare*, cheek-to-cheek
like the rubbing of stones together.

I could make love to you until skin wears away,
flesh upon flesh, sinew to sinew, bone of your bone.

Your fragrance on my fingers and hair,
stained sheets, blood red poppies.

Vertigo, Approaching Corniglia

*"...the words fall lightly between us,
I look at you in a soft quivering."*
—Eugenio Montale

We devour foccacia in Vernazza,
pomodori i mozzarella,

stock up on aqua minerale
a break before the next leg.

Greasy men peddle rooms to backpackers,
hungry women stare through me.

You feed me on steps in the harbor,
a freckled smile, sixteen again, forgives.

Trails necklace the mountains, blue sky,
wind in the branches, our footsteps.

The past follows me like a mumbling old man,
how I left you on a ledge outside San Francisco,

cold calls in Chicago, phone disconnected.
I was married and alone, an olive black heart on ice.

Dizzy on the edges, I grab the mountain.
How far had I fallen in Siena, Montecatini, Lucca?

We could train it from here to the end of the line,
call it a day, stay friends, but there's no distance

between our villages. Hearts ripen without destination.
How far had I fallen like petals into the sea?

A journey in the touch of your hand.
Love, like fresh garlic, simmers on a low flame.

Sauce from Scratch, Manarola

*"Pick up dirt from the old trail pilgrim,
and throw it to the wind."*
       –Charles Wright

Garlic mulled in wooden bowls,
our footfall on the trail,

you squeeze my heart like a ripe tomato.
Pulp drips from your fingers down your arms.

Our laundry hangs from lemon trees,
stained by old lovers, drying in the sun.

Love is the silence that lurks
underneath the tongue, scared to death.

We spread olive oil in the pan,
add pork chops, carrots, a pinch of sugar,

stir it on low heat for hours, taste spoonfuls,
careful not to burn the onions.

Peeling skins from your clove
I search for answers: Will you hurt me again?

Will this be forgotten when we get back home?
Your mind shifts like plates along a fault line,

difficult footing, lost in each others lives.
Your boots creased, beaten from hikes,

worn like portobello mushrooms.
This is their last excursion.

In Manarola, you will leave them with the farmer's wife.
I break new boots in, climb back into your life.

Last Words, Riomaggiore

*"A few instants have scorched everything we are: all but two faces,
two masks which, with a struggle, carve themselves into a smile."*
—Eugenio Montale

Thirsty, sweating, lost
we ask for directions

to the Avenue of Love,
one last stretch of road

from Manarola to Riomaggiore.
Bushels of hearts kiss walls

with graffiti. Old men on benches
gawk as you pass.

We hiked through terraced vineyards,
poplars, cypress, sunflowers,

mountains, blue seas below us,
and nothing more beautiful

than your freckled shoulders.
Our years apart smell

like fresh basil roasting
in the sun, seasoned hearts

gored by the world.
I swore I'd never fall again.

When this journey ends,
tell my children, my friends

this is where I tumbled into the ocean.
Please scatter my ashes

like crushed red pepper
on the Via Dell' Amore.

www.ingramcontent.com/pod-product-compliance
Lightning Source LLC
Chambersburg PA
CBHW032049290426
44110CB00012B/1019